SCIENCE VIEW

HEAT & ENERGY

©2005 by Chelsea House Publishers, a subsidiary of Haights Cross Communications.

A Haights Cross Communications ⌐ Company

Printed and bound in China.
10 9 8 7 6 5 4 3 2 1

Library of Congress Cataloging-in-Publication Data applied for.

ISBN: 0-7910-8207-5

Chelsea House Publishers

2080 Cabot Blvd. West, Suite 201
Langhorne, PA 19047-1813

http://www.chelseahouse.com

Produced by

David West ⚇ Children's Books
7 Princeton Court
55 Felsham Road
London SW15 1AZ

Designer: Rob Shone
Editor: Gail Bushnell
Picture Research: Carlotta Cooper

PHOTO CREDITS :
Abbreviations: t-top, m-middle, b-bottom, r-right, l-left, c-center.

Front cover - tl & r, bl & m - Corbis Images. Pages 3 & 10–11, 4–5 & 18r, 6 both, 8t, 8–9, 10, 12l, 13t, 15r, 16, 16–17 both, 21, 24, 26t, 27t & m - Corbis Images. 7l, 20 - DPMU0399 Images @ 1999 Photodisc, Inc. 7tr - Daewoo Electronics Sales UK. 11b - Solar & Heliospheric Observatory /www.soho.nascom.nasa.gov. 19 - NASA. 24–25, 25t - Stock Images. 25m - National Oceanic & Atmospheric Administration (NOAA). 28 - Rex Features Ltd.

With special thanks to the models: Felix Blom, Tucker Bryant and Margaux Monfared.

An explanation of difficult words can be found in the glossary on page 31.

SCIENCE VIEW

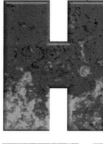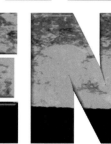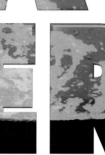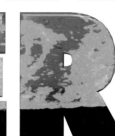

HEAT & ENERGY

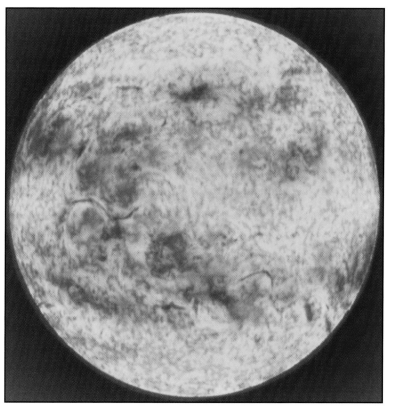

Steve Parker

CHELSEA HOUSE
PUBLISHERS

A Haights Cross Communications Company

CONTENTS

WARNING!
All projects should be supervised by a responsible adult. Some need extra care and expert help, and are marked with a red box. Make sure the instructions are followed. *Never take risks.*

INTRODUCTION

Phew, this summer has been scorching! But it's better than wintertime, which can be freezing. We have to turn on the radiators and make warm drinks. Heat is very important in daily life. It keeps us and our surroundings comfortable, cooks our foods, is vital in industry, and, with moisture, it encourages wildlife to thrive.

How it **WORKS**

These panels explain the science behind the projects, and the processes and principles that we see every day, but which we may not always understand!

PROJECTS

The projects are simple to do with supervision, using household items. Remember–scientists are cautious. They prepare equipment thoroughly, they know what should happen, and they *always* put safety first.

Water trickling underground is boiled by great heat deep in the Earth's rocks. The hot water and steam spurt out as a geyser.

Energy causes change and makes things happen. When heat is present, this often causes change–depending on what is hot.

HEAT AND HAPPENINGS

We cannot see heat directly. A flame has heat, but what we see is its light energy. However, we can see events that happen due to heat. These events may be changes in the form of a substance, like ice melting to water. They may be movements, such as the motion of a steam locomotive or jet engine. Or they may be the destructive change known as burning or combustion.

Burning is a chemical change or reaction between a substance (here natural gas) and oxygen in air.

A rocket burns fuel with oxygen to create white-hot gases. Space lacks oxygen, so the rocket takes its own in chemical form.

CHANGING FORMS

Another feature of energy is that it can be altered or converted from one form to another. So, heat can be made from other energy forms, like movement, electricity, and chemicals, and also converted into them.

NO LOSS OR GAIN

Energy can be converted, but it is never lost or gained. The total amount of energy is conserved– it remains the same. The principle of energy conservation is extremely important in all areas of science.

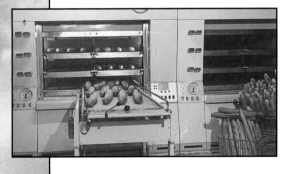

In baking, some heat is stored in chemical form in bread. The rest conducts through the oven walls to the surroundings.

How it **WORKS**

The metal is hotter than the water, so heat moves to raise the water temperature. Ice is colder, so heat moves from the water to melt it, lowering the water temperature. In both cases, heat moves, but the total amount of heat energy stays the same.

Heat flows out from hot metal

Heat flows into cold ice

MOVING BUT CONSERVED

Thermometer

Heated metal

Ice cubes

Heat naturally spreads from hot objects to cold ones. Put a warm metal object and ice cubes in separate glasses of cool water. Take the water temperature each minute.

THE BIGGEST HEATER

Deep below Earth's surface, rocks are so hot, they are melted. We see them when a volcano erupts. However, this heat is tiny compared to the heat from our nearest star–the Sun.

FUSION POWER

The temperature at the Earth's center is 9,900°F (5,500°C)–but at the core of the Sun it is 27 million°F (15 million°C)! The Sun glows almost white-hot by changing the very light substance hydrogen into slightly heavier helium. As this happens, hydrogen atoms join or fuse and tiny parts of them are destroyed, releasing heat, light, and other energy.

The Sun's surface has a temperature of 10,800°F (6,000°C). It "boils" continuously with incredible heat coming from the core, throwing out giant swirls of flames.

Although people enjoy sunbathing, the Sun's ultraviolet (UV) rays can be harmful and cause skin cancer.

WARMTH FOR LIFE

n a second, the Sun gives out heat energy equivalent to 90 trillion nuclear explosions. The solar heat reaching Earth warms our planet to an average yearly temperature of 59°F (15°C), with some regions up to 122°F (50°C). Without the Sun, our temperature would plunge to –454°F (–270°C) and all life would cease.

A solar furnace receives the Sun's heat reflected from hundreds of mirrors and can reach 18,000°F (10,000°C).

SOLAR OVEN

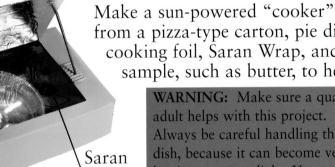

Make a sun-powered "cooker" from a pizza-type carton, pie dish, cooking foil, Saran Wrap, and a sample, such as butter, to heat.

Saran Wrap

Foil

Cardboard box

WARNING: Make sure a qualified adult helps with this project. Always be careful handling the pie dish, because it can become very hot in strong sunlight. Use potholders for protection.

How it WORKS

The Sun's heat and light shine straight into the cooking area and also reflect into it from the shiny lid. As the heat builds up, the Saran Wrap keeps it in the box, just as glass retains warmth in a greenhouse.

Sun's rays

Trapped heat

Satellites traveling close to the Sun have special heat-proof covers.

11

Ovens, central heating, light bulbs, car engines, candles– sources of heat are all around.

Natural gas fuel contains many kinds of hydrocarbons that burn well in air.

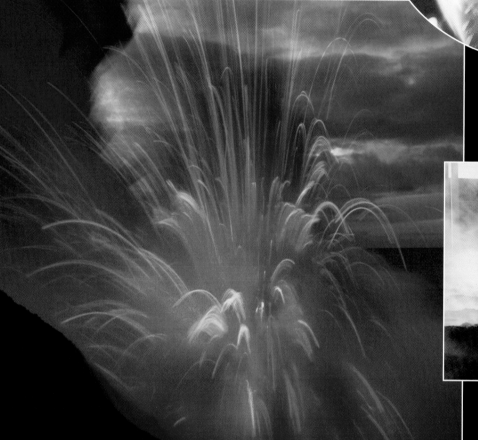

Fiery fumes, red-hot ash, and molten rock heated deep in the Earth erupt from a volcano.

NATURAL HEAT

Some sources of energy are converted or changed into heat by natural processes. The inside of the Earth is still very hot from its formation long ago and the crushing forces deep in the rocks. This geothermal (Earth-heat) energy melts rock into the red-hot, liquid lava that bursts from volcanoes and turns underground water into scalding steam.

How it WORKS

Fuels like gasoline, diesel and natural gas contain linked hydrogen and carbon atoms, called hydrocarbons. Burning makes these react with the oxygen in air to break the bonds, form carbon dioxide gas and water, and release energy as heat and light.

MOVING HEAT

Any moving object has kinetic energy, and this can be changed into heat. As machine parts wear, rub, and scrape together, they get hot. Lubricating oil not only lets them move smoothly, it also carries away some of the heat.

Rubbing or friction changes kinetic (moving) energy into heat, like these hot sparks from a grinding machine.

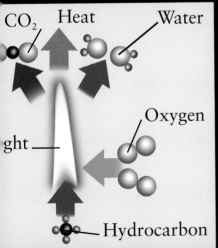

Decay makes heat, as in compost heaps, and when manure rots into fertilizer.

CO_2 Heat   Water

Oxygen

ght

Hydrocarbon

HIGH-ENERGY FUELS

Fuels like gasoline and coal contain lots of energy in the links or bonds that hold their atoms together. As the fuel burns, the atoms separate and the chemical bond energy changes into heat. In a nuclear reactor, the centers, or nuclei, of atoms split apart, releasing heat and radioactive energy.

Vast quantities of heat are generated in the reactor of a nuclear power station. The used fuel is very hot and is stored in large cooling ponds.

13

Heat is a form of energy. Temperature is a measure of the level, or degree, of this energy. However, temperature is more complex than it seems.

TOTAL AMOUNT

The depth of a pond alone does not show the total amount of water it contains. Similarly, the temperature of an object alone does not measure the total amount of heat energy it contains. Extra information is needed, such as the weight or mass of the object.

RELATIVE AMOUNTS

Despite its limits, temperature is a useful measure in everyday life. It compares relative levels of heat in various objects and substances, and shows degrees of heat loss and gain. We measure a huge variety of temperatures–when cooking, in machines and industrial processes, in conditions for plants and animals, for weather, and even in our bodies.

Coolers keep food fresher. Their temperature is taken often. If it rises, food may "go bad" and decay, causing illness.

Some thermometers contain a liquid that enlarges or expands with heat, along the scale.

THERMOMETER

A thermometer can be made from dyed water, a cork with a hole, a straw, and two plastic bottles. A ring of cardboard holds the small bottle inside the larger one. Make a cardboard scale to show the water level.

Plastic bottles
Cardboard support
Cork
Straw
Cardboard scale
Dyed water

A thermometer that switches a heating system on and off is called a thermostat. It keeps temperature constant, as in this greenhouse.

TEMPERATURE SCALES

Temperatures are measured by devices called thermometers. In daily life we use degrees Fahrenheit, °F, but scientists use the Kelvin scale, K. A rise of 1 K equals 1.8°F, but the Kelvin scale starts at the lowest temperature possible, absolute zero. 0 K is the same as −459.67°F (−273.15°C).

How it WORKS

Put the thermometer out in the sunshine and watch the water level descend on the scale! The Sun's heat warms the air in the upper bottle. This gets bigger or expands (page 18) into the straw, pushing the water level down. Try putting the thermometer in the refrigerator!

The planet Mercury is so close to the Sun, its "day" temperature is 842°F (450°C). "Night" on the other, dark side is −274°F (−170°C)!

15

HEAT AND STATE

A ship floats on the very common substance we call water. However, it may be sunk by water, too–if that water is frozen into an iceberg.

THREE STATES

Water is a liquid. It can flow and change shape. Liquid is one of three forms a substance can take, called states. The other states are solid, like iron and glass, and gas, such as oxygen and nitrogen in air.

DEPENDING ON HEAT

The state of a substance depends on how much heat it contains, as indicated by its temperature. Water is liquid at everyday temperatures, but if its heat is taken away, its state changes. It turns into hard ice, or solidifies. If ice receives heat, it changes back into liquid water, known as melting.

Water is the most common everyday substance that exists in all three states– seen here as a liquid.

Water heated to more than 212°F (100°C) deep underground emerges as a gas mixed with tiny droplets–steam.

If enough heat is taken away to reduce water's temperature below 32°F (0°C), it freezes into ice, like these icicles.

How it WORKS

Squeezing or pressure causes changes of state, too. Great pressure on ice causes heat at the point of contact, making it melt. A skate blade melts the ice momentarily as it passes. So, ice skaters should really be called "water skaters."

Downward pressure of skater melts ice

Metal blade
Thin water layer
Ice

GIVE AND TAKE AWAY

More heat makes water change state again into gas, or water vapor. This happens when water boils into steam. Almost all substances can exist as solid, liquid, or gas, mostly at extreme temperatures. Rocks do not melt until they reach 1,800°F (1,000°C).

In the cold ice-hockey arena, the players' speed depends on tiny patches of heat (right).

SLICE THE ICE

Here's how to slice ice in two as if you were cutting butter. Wedge an ice cube into a bottle neck. Join two weights by a piece of thin wire. Drape the wire over the ice cube, and wait. Slowly, the wire cuts down through the ice. In the freezer, the "cut" may "heal" itself!

Ice cube

Bottle

Wire

Weight

17

Air expands with heat, too. The hot air in a balloon is lighter, for its volume, than the air around it, and so it rises.

Thermometers, heating controls, car engine cooling systems, buckled railroad tracks in summer–these all happen when objects are heated and get bigger.

CHANGE IN HEAT = CHANGE IN SIZE

Heat makes the tiny atoms of an object or substance move, or vibrate, more. As this happens, they also move slightly farther apart, making the whole object bigger. This effect is called expansion. As heat is taken away from an object and it becomes colder, the reverse happens. It gets slightly smaller, known as contraction.

A barrel's metal hoops are heated before being put over the wooden slats. The hoops cool, contract, and squeeze the slats tight.

EXPANSION RATES

The rate of expansion varies between different substances. In general, metals expand faster than nonmetals. Some metals, however, expand faster than others and are used in thermostats.

FIT TO BUST

Expansion is usually tiny, but it can cause trouble. Railroad tracks expand in hot weather, so they need spaces between them to prevent buckling. Planes that fly at supersonic speeds get very hot and may expand an inch or two.

How it **WORKS**

A thermostat contains a strip of two different metals. As it warms, one metal expands faster. This bends the strip and breaks the electrical contact to turn off the heating.

Contact
Copper
Steel
Heat
Contact broken
Copper expands more

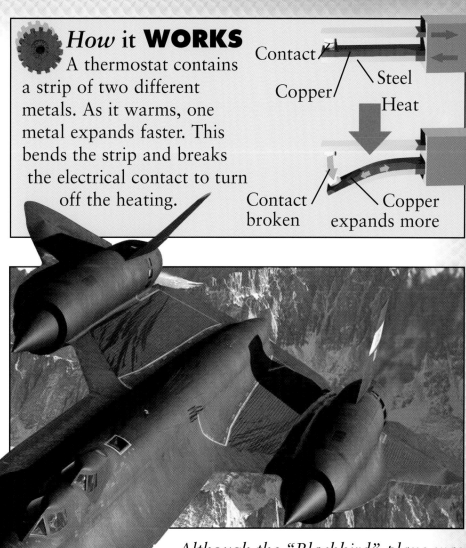

Although the "Blackbird" plane was made of titanium metal, which expands little with heat, it still had tiny expansion gaps. This meant that at supersonic speeds, when it got very hot, the parts fit together perfectly.

EXPANSION METER

By using an expansion meter, you can see a wire get longer with heat. A hanging weight rests on the end of the pointer, behind the pivot. Heat the wire with a hairdryer and watch the pointer rise up the scale.

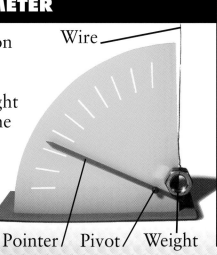

Wire

Pointer / Pivot / Weight

How it **WORKS**

The wire warms and lengthens. This lowers the weight on the pointer's short end, so its longer end pivots up the scale. Repeat the test for copper wire, steel wire, cotton thread, and plastic cord.

Heat expands wire
Weight lowers
Heat
Pointer rises

How it WORKS
A warm drink loses heat in all three ways. The heat energy conducts into the spoon and, to a lesser extent, the mug. It is convected away by moving air. It also radiates from all the warm surfaces as infrared or "heat" rays.

The flames of a fire lose much of their heat as radiation, as "heat" or infrared rays that spread outward from them.

You can feel the warm air from a fire, and see the glow, but don't touch or you'll be burned!

WAYS TO TRAVEL

Heat moves from place to place in three ways. First, conduction happens when two objects are in contact and heat seeps or flows between them. The second way, convection, is when a gas such as air takes up heat from a hot object and moves or flows, carrying the heat energy with it. Liquids such as water flow and carry heat by convection.

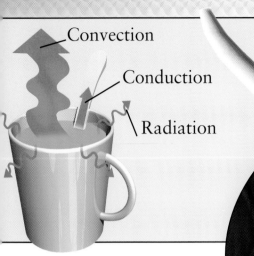

Convection

Conduction

Radiation

The walls of a furnace get very hot as conduction allows heat to seep through them from the interior.

Sun-warmed air expands and flows upward. Gliders use these convection currents to lift them higher.

THE THIRD WAY

Heat also moves as rays or waves called infrared radiation. These rays are made of magnetic and electrical energy, similar to light rays. Often, we see a mix of infrared and light as the glow of a hot object.

MOVING THROUGH NOTHING

Both conduction and convection need an object or substance for the heat to travel. Radiation does not. Infrared waves can travel through the nothingness of a vacuum. This is just as well, because space is a vacuum, and the Sun's heat (and light) pass through it to Earth.

21

Gloves keep our hands warm in cool weather, and also keep our hands cool when we touch warm objects. How?

A car's exhaust system conducts away some of the engine's heat and "glows" at very high temperatures.

STOPPING HEAT

Heat flows through and between substances by conduction (see previous page). Some substances allow heat through very easily, and are conductors. Other substances, like the material of gloves, carry heat very badly. They are known as insulators.

A motorcycle engine has metal cooling fins (see inset). Their large surface area conducts the engine's heat away to the air.

BEAD RACE

Pour some hot water into a bowl. Put a plastic stick, metal knife, and wooden spoon in the bowl. Stick a small bead to each with butter. Watch to see which bead slides down the fastest.

How it WORKS

The best conductor carries heat the fastest to melt the butter and release the bead. Materials that do not conduct heat are good insulators. A thermos's stopper stops heat conduction. The vacuum also prevents conduction, as well as convection. The silvered sides prevent radiation.

Stopper

Vacuum

Silvered glass

Warm air rises, so much heat is lost through a house roof. Fiber-type insulation cuts the loss.

SLOWER

Most metals are good heat or thermal conductors. Wood, plastic, glass, ceramic, and fabric are thermal insulators. These materials are used to control heat's flow and movement in cars, cookers, clothes, houses, and even space rockets.

INTENSE HEAT

A spacecraft returning to Earth reenters the atmosphere at great speed. Friction with the air creates intense heat, over 2,880°F (1,600°C). Special insulation on the craft keeps it from burning up.

The space shuttle has high-performance insulating tiles on its underside.

23

The Sun's heat provides far more than warm summer days. It produces winds, clouds, and the rest of weather.

PATCHY HEAT

Some areas of the Earth's surface, like dark rocks, soak up more heat than others. This difference causes patchy heating of the air, too. Warm air rises, cool air moves along to take its place, and the result is wind.

Clouds swirl in winds across our world–all due to the energy of the Sun's heat.

Billions of tiny water droplets in clouds are raised by solar heat and fall due to gravity.

BLOWING ALONG

The Sun's warmth also turns water in lakes, rivers, and oceans into vapor in the air. This powers the water cycle. And as winds blow, they cause ripples on water. At sea, the ripples build into huge waves that crash on the shore and wear away the land. So, solar heat even shapes our coastlines.

WATER CYCLE

***How* it WORKS**
Solar heat energy evaporates water–changes it to invisible water vapor, which is warm and rises into the air. This moist air blows up mountains, where conditions are colder. The cooled moisture condenses, or turns back into water, as droplets that form clouds, mist, rain, sleet, and snow.

In a drought, the Sun's warmth evaporates a lake's water and then cracks the mud with its heat.

LIFE'S NEEDS

Life thrives best in warm, damp places like tropical rain forests. The Sun's heat brings the warmth directly, and the moisture indirectly, through the water cycle. Without them, living things would perish.

Lack of heat means water falls as frozen flakes of snow. Blizzards, gales, and extreme weather affect daily life.

Sun

4 Cooled vapor forms clouds and rain.

3 Moist air rises and cools.

5 Rain fills rivers.

2 Moist air moves inland.

1 Sun's heat evaporates water in seas, lakes, and rivers.

6 Rivers flow to sea.

Make a simple "water cycle" with a plastic sheet, bowl, and tumbler. Leave in a warm place. Heat evaporates the water, which condenses on the plastic's underside and runs down to the tumbler.

Plastic with weight in center to form a cone shape

Tumbler

Water in bowl

BODY HEAT

Some animals make their own heat to stay warm. Others are at the mercy of their surroundings.

SLOW-BURNING BODIES

Birds and mammals are "warm-blooded." Some of the energy contained in their food, in chemical form, is changed by a "slow-burn" process in the body to release heat gradually. So, birds and mammals can stay warm and active even in cold places like polar regions and high on mountains. However, they also have ways of keeping cool in hot weather.

Great activity in hot conditions creates a risk of overheating. Splashes of water aid sweat to help cool the body.

EVAPORATION

Our body temperature should be 98.6°F (37°C). A rise, hyperthermia, can be very harmful. The body reacts by sweating. Tiny beads of sweat ooze onto the skin. See how sweat works with two thermometers. Wrap the bulb of one with wet cotton. Blow them both with a hairdryer set on "cool." Which cools fastest?

Many mammals cannot sweat effectively because of their fur, so they pant away the heat instead.

In frozen Antarctica, penguins have both thick feathers and blubber to hold in body heat.

Reptiles like the iguana lizard become less active as conditions get cooler.

STAYING WARM

To prevent heat loss from their bodies, "warm-blooded" animals have insulation. Birds have feathers and mammals have fur. In the water, a furry covering would be soggy and ineffective. So, full-time water mammals like whales have a thick layer of insulating fat, called blubber, under the skin.

COLD-BLOODED

Nearly all other animals, like snakes, fish, and insects, are "cold-blooded." Their bodies remain very similar in temperature to their surroundings. In cold weather, they hardly move and hide away for safety.

Read temperature on scale

Uncovered bulb

Wet cotton around bulb

How it WORKS

Water needs warmth to evaporate into vapor. As air blows on the thermometers, the water in the cotton draws heat from its bulb to evaporate. So, the reading on this thermometer is lower than on the other one. Sweat cools the body in the same way.

Fall in temperature

Wet cotton

Heat   Air

Fires rage when wind brings continuing supplies of fresh oxygen-rich air to fan the flames.

Objects with a temperature above about 122°F (50°C) feel hot. This warns us to keep clear, since heat burns our bodies and smoke harms our airways and lungs. Fires kill–so beware!

STARVED OF OXYGEN

Flames, like animals, must have oxygen to survive. This gas makes up one-fifth of air. It takes part in the chemical reaction of combustion, or burning (see page 8). Prevent oxygen from reaching a fire, using foam, a blanket, or a heavy gas like carbon dioxide, and the flames "suffocate."

HELP!

Some fire extinguishers use these various methods of preventing oxygen from reaching a fire. Fires can also be put out by removing the heat from the flames, by using water. Fires will also go out if they have no more fuel left to burn.

Spraying foam on a fire prevents oxygen in the air from reaching it, so the flames soon go out.

In remote places, such as forests, planes and helicopters are used to drop water or fire-retardant chemicals directly onto wildfires.

SNUFFED OUT

Put a small votive candle on a support in a bowl of water. Carefully place a heat-proof glass over it. Gradually, the flame shrinks and goes out.

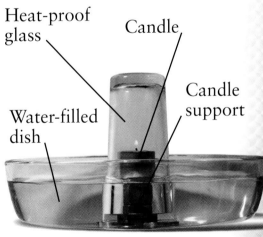

Heat-proof glass

Candle

Candle support

Water-filled dish

How it WORKS

The covered candle can only burn using oxygen in the glass. Once consumed, the flame dies. Also, water is pushed up into the glass to replace the lost oxygen.

Oxygen-less air

Extinguished candle flame

Rise in water level

Air pressure

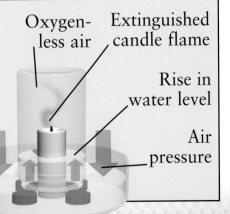

WARNING: Make sure a qualified adult helps with this project. Always be careful when lighting the candle and placing the glass over it. Allow the glass to cool before removing it.

TEMPERATURE SCALES–°F AND °C

The everyday temperature scale is degrees Fahrenheit, °F. This is based on two set points, the melting point of ice to water and the boiling point of water to steam. The temperature difference between them is divided into 100 units, from 32°F (0°C) to 212°F (100°C).
• To change °F to °C–subtract 32 from °F, multiply by 5, then divide by 9.
• To change °C to °F–multiply °C by 9, divide by 5, then add 32.

TEMPERATURE SCALE–K

The scientific scale of temperature is Kelvin (without the word *degrees* or the symbol °). A temperature difference of 33.8°F (1°C) is the same as the difference of 1 K. However, the scales start at different places, with 0 K being absolute zero.

ABSOLUTE ZERO

The coldest possible temperature anywhere in the universe is absolute zero, when atoms and molecules stop moving altogether and so have no energy of motion or heat.
Absolute zero
• 0 K = –459.67°F = –273.15°C

JOULES AND CALORIES

Any kind of energy, including heat, can be measured in units known as joules. A standard one-kilowatt electric heater gives out up to 1,000 joules per second. The human body produces around 80–130 joules per second while asleep or resting. (Heat and other forms of energy, such as chemical energy in foods, can be measured in calories. One calorie equals 4.2 joules.)

MELTING AND BOILING POINTS

Here are some examples of melting points (MPs) and boiling points (BPs):

• Oxygen	MP –360.4°F (–218°C)	BP 287.4°F (–183°C)
• Alcohol	MP –173.2°F (–114°C)	BP 172.9°F (78.3°C)
• Mercury	MP –37.8°F (–38.8°C)	BP 673.9°F (356.6°C)
• Cooking oil	MP –4°F (–20°C)	BP 392°F (200+°C)
• Water	MP 32°F (0°C)	BP 212°F (100°C)
• Aluminum	MP 1,220°F (660°C)	BP 4,472.6°F (2,467°C)
• Iron	MP 2,795°F (1,535°C)	BP 4,982°F (2,750°C)
• Titanium	MP 3,020°F (1,660°C)	BP 5,948.6°F (3,287°C)

Mercury is used in standard thermometers and alcohol in low-temperature ones, due to the temperature ranges when they expand.

TEMPERATURE RANGES

900 million°F (500 million°C)	Scientific research into plasmas
27 million°F (15 million°C)	Center of the Sun
10, 800°F (6,000°C)	Surface of the Sun
9,900°F (5,500°C)	Center of the Earth
1,832°F (1,000°C)	Lava (molten rock)
428°F (220°C)	High cooking temperature
212°F (100°C)	Boiling point of water
136.4°F (58°C)	Hottest weather (Libya)
122°F (50°C)	Hot bathwater
98.6°F (37°C)	Human body
68–75°F (20–25°C)	Room temperature
41°F (5°C)	Typical refrigerator
32°F (0°C)	Melting point of water
–22°F (–30°C)	Typical freezer
–109.3°F (–78.5°C)	"Dry ice" (solid carbon dioxide)
–128.5°F (–89.2°C)	Coldest weather (Antarctica)
–328°F (–200°C)	Liquid nitrogen (ultracold or cryogenic storage)
–459.67°F (–273.15°C)	Absolute zero

GLOSSARY

atom
The smallest particle of an element, made up of a central nucleus surrounded by electrons.

boil
To change a liquid into a gas, usually by adding heat.

combustion
The process of burning, in which a chemical substance combines with oxygen to produce heat (and usually light, too).

condense
To change from a gas to a liquid, usually by taking away heat.

conduction
When energy, such as heat or electricity, moves through an object or from one object to another.

convection
Movement of heat through a liquid or gas by currents, as when rising air carries heat with it.

evaporate
To change from a liquid to a vapor or gas.

geothermal
"Earth heat" or "ground heat"–the vast quantities of heat deep inside the Earth.

melt
To change from a solid to a liquid, usually by adding heat. Molten means "melted."

radiation
Energy sent out or given off, usually in the form of electro-magnetic waves, such as radio waves, infrared or heat, and light.

solar
Having to do with the Sun. Solar energy is a mixture of heat, light, and other energy radiated by the Sun.

solidify
To change from a liquid to a solid, usually by taking away heat.

31